RISE UP, *Princess*

60 DAYS TO REVEALING YOUR ROYAL IDENTITY

BY KRISTEN DALTON WOLFE

FOUNDER OF SHEISMORE.COM & A MISS USA

Rise Up, Princess
60 Days to Revealing Your Royal Identity

Copyright 2014 by Wolfe Pack Media LLC

Written By: Kristen Dalton Wolfe
Formatted By: Jane Kennedy
Cover Art By: Leah Gunn
Edited By: Kris Wolfe

SheisMore.com
Facebook.com/SheisMore
Pinterest.com/SheisMore
Twitter.com/SheisMore
Instagram: She_is_More

Printed in U.S.A

This devotional is dedicated to my incredible husband, Kris.
Thank you for standing by me and supporting me on this
God-appointed journey to fulfill my dreams. You are my rock
and best friend. I love you!

This devotional is also dedicated to my mother, Jeannine, who
truly embodies what it means to be a royal daughter of the
King and to my sisters, Kenzie and Julia, for giving me the big
sister's heart to reach all young girls and women. Each of you
have inspired me to write and finish this book.

A Special Note from *Kristen* :

You can do this journey solo or invite a few girlfriends to grab a devotional and go through it together. That way, you can hold each other accountable, have some beautiful discussions and grow even more through expressing and listening to one another's thoughts and feelings! " As iron sharpens iron, so a friend sharpens a friend." Proverbs 27:17

The scriptures used in this devotional are based on a variety of biblical translations.

Disclaimer: The content in this devotional, although rooted in biblical scripture, are the expressed interpretations of Kristen Dalton Wolfe. She is not a licensed professional.

Table of Contents

She Reveals:

She Radiates:

She Reigns:

Dear *Princess,*

I am so excited and blessed to share this devotional with you. I was raised in a Christian home, going to church every Sunday, was actively involved in youth group, bible study and mission trips. As the oldest of four children, my definition for success was performance and approval. I never felt beautiful, I wasn't comfortable in my own skin, I dealt with painful cystic acne, loneliness and depression. I believed if I could win Miss USA, I would finally feel worthy, beautiful, and all my insecurities would disappear.

In 2009, my childhood dream came true of winning Miss USA. As incredibly exciting as it was, it wasn't the magical cure I thought it would be. I doubted myself all the time, I wanted to please everyone and spent many nights crying alone on the bathroom floor of my NYC titleholder apartment. I soon found that there is only emptiness in seeking the affirmation of a title, accolade, or people to give me identity.

One day, someone spoke words to me that changed my life forever. I was doubting my purpose in life and my friend said to me, "Kristen, don't you know that you are a daughter of the One True King?" I had never heard or even thought of that before. But yes, he was right. This was relational, eye-opening, and a complete paradigm shift to the way I had been seeing myself and living. This meant I was *royalty.* This meant I was His *Princess.* This meant I was born for royal purpose.

You are His Princess too. You have a royal identity no title or worldly crown could ever give you or take away. When we accept Our King's hand, our former nature and old ways melt away and transform into an everlasting royal identity that gives us a life with unshakable access to His power and confidence.

You are embarking on a 60 day journey that will give you the power to start walking as the Princess you were designed to be. You will:

1. Start to see yourself the way that God sees you,
2. Realize that your past doesn't define you,
3. Believe you are here on purpose for a great purpose and
4. Build the confidence to bring your royal mission to its' full completion.

She Reveals. She Radiates. She Reigns. This is your time. Rise Up, Princess.

From one princess to another,

Kristen

Introduction

In my reign as Miss USA, I met so many young women and girls who opened their hearts, revealed their dreams, fears and insecurities to me. I wanted to take each girl home. I wanted to sit down and tell them everything they needed to know that would empower them to rise above their current circumstances. I knew I needed to reach girls and women on a larger scale. I wanted to get resources, inspiration and encouragement to as many ladies as I could at one time so there wouldn't be one more girl who lost her life to circumstances, culture, or her family tree. Thus, SheisMore.com was born and my dream of reaching women worldwide came true.

In the time I have been writing and speaking through SheisMore.com, I've had the blessing of meeting and mentoring many young women who have been through heartache, hurt, and have felt their royal identities stripped away. Since I was a child, I knew God wanted me to write a book, but I didn't know if I had anything of value to say. I didn't know if I had the ability or the credibility to really help anyone.

After going to Australia on a speaking tour, my heart was pierced by the plethora of girls, Christian and non-Christian alike, who were hurting. They carried so much shame and deep insecurities to the point of self-harm. It reminded me that even those of us who know the stories of the Bible, who are involved in church culture, and sing praise and worship songs, still don't truly know how God sees them. I realized that I did indeed have a valuable message to share.

Throughout my Christian life, I have read countless devotionals and faith-based inspirational books. They have all helped me in seasons of life and helped shape me into who I am today. Out of all of those books, devotionals, tapes, and workshops, I have combined the top three elements that carry the most power and impact to create *Rise Up, Princess*. This devotional **speaks out** the promises, beauty and truth from **God's Word** through **declarations** and **gratitude.**

Rise Up Princess is composed of 60 daily power prayers to your King using the three power elements: Gratitude, Declarations, and the Word. On this journey, you are committing to discover your Royal Identity in three phases of 20 days each:

she *reveals:*

Unveil falsely held beliefs and replace them with God's truths.

she *radiates:*

Embrace the light within you and radiate the true beauty you are.

she *reigns:*

Understand you were set apart on purpose and gain the confidence to embark on your royal purpose.

The Three Elements that Make this Journey Powerful

Gratitude: Often times in prayer, we beg and ask for things as if we don't already have them. But God has already given us everything we could ask, hope for, or imagine before we were even born. Since we already have inherited all the blessings we need, the most powerful prayer is to thank God for what He says he has already given you before you have seen it with your eyes. "*For we live by faith, not by sight.*" 2 Corinthians 5:7

Hebrews 11:1 says, "*Now faith is the reality of what is hoped for, the proof of what is not seen.*" When you thank God in advance for His blessings, you will start to live expectantly of them. Just as a pregnant woman starts to live and prepare for motherhood as she is waiting in expectancy for the birth of her child, you should live and prepare for the blessings, dreams and future God has for you with a thankful heart. **He has already given us everything we ask for in the heavenly realms. It is a matter of awakening our hearts to the gifts, plans, hope and future He wants to manifest here on Earth.** "*Set your mind on the things above, not the things that are here on earth.*" Colossians 3:2

Declaration: There is power in our thought life and the words we speak. The Word of God and behavioral psychology are in alignment in telling us to think, speak and act in order for something to be. Job 22:28 says, "*Decree a thing and it shall be established for you; and light will shine on your ways.*" I believe that a common mistake many Christians make is believing that once they accept Jesus as Lord, their lives will magically transform forever without changing anything in their lives. But change starts in our minds. We have to make a conscious choice all the time to think on, speak on and declare good things to happen. Hebrews 11:3 explains the power in our words: "*By faith we understand that the worlds were prepared by the word of God, so that what is seen was not made out of things which are visible.*" **In this devotional, you will make daily declaration over your identity, your precious worth and destiny.**

The Word: *"Your word is a lamp for my feet, a light on my path."* Psalms 119:105. Declarations and a thankful faithfulness are meaningless if they are not rooted in scripture. It is written in Hebrews 4:12 that God's Word is quick, powerful and sharper than any two-edged sword, piercing to the division of soul and spirit and discerning of our thoughts and intents of our hearts. I can't even tell you the power you will experience in your life when you recite God's description of you and His promises over your life as opposed to positive affirmations you make up or read in a book.

In *Rise Up, Princess*, you will declare and thank God for the Princess he made you to be using the God-breathed Word.

I pray that this journey is transformative. Consistency and commitment are key elements to reaping your fullest benefits. Your relationship with God will flourish and overflow through your conversations and quality time you spend with Him in this devotional. He wants to hear from you. He longs to listen to your heart.

Additionally, there is a status update challenge for each day. This is a beautiful way for you to inspire other women all over that it is time for them to #RiseUp too. Simply copy the status update and send it out through social media, being sure to tag @SheisMore and #RiseUpPrincess.

Instagram is @She_is_More

she

Reveals

her true identity

DAY 1

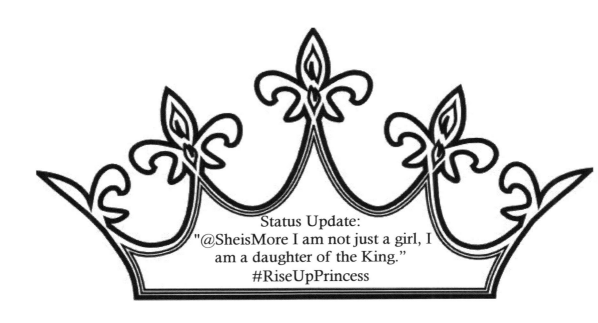

Status Update:
"@SheisMore I am not just a girl, I
am a daughter of the King."
#RiseUpPrincess

So you are no longer a slave, but God's child;
and since you are his child, God has made
you also an heir.
Galatians 4:7

My Father and my King,

Thank You that I am not just any girl who found Christianity. Thank You that I am not limited to serving or performing in order to gain approval. You made me for so much more than that. You intended for me to be Your precious daughter. You designed me for relationship and honest intimacy with You. You invite me to crawl up on Your lap whenever I want. I can reveal the secrets of my heart and the sorrows in my soul when I spend time with You.

Thank You God that I am no longer a slave to fitting in. I don't have to strive to be the perfect Christian. I had it in reverse all along. Because I am Your child, the daughter You love, I already have the DNA to be like You. When I remove the layers of culture, familial and spiritual damage, the girl I see in the mirror is a reflection of love, creativity, joy, wonder and peace.

Today, I declare all barriers have evaporated between us and I will participate in a royal relationship with You. I will no longer hide in fear and I will open my heart to You in prayer, conversation and gratitude. I am reclaiming my royal identity today.

Your Princess,

Amen.

DAY 2

Status Update: "@SheisMore I have royalty in my veins and lead with integrity." #RiseUpPrincess

But you are a chosen people, a royal priesthood, a holy nation, God's special possession, that you may declare the praises of him who called you out of darkness into his wonderful light.
1 Peter 2:9

My King and Royal Father,

I always dreamed of exploring a King's Palace. Thank You, my Majesty for inviting me to be seated next to You. I used to imagine being a princess as a little girl. I never realized that I already *am* one! I am Your daughter and You are the King of the Universe.

You say I am chosen, I am royal, I am a saint and I am holy. Your definition of me trumps the labels that others have ever spoken over me. You say that I am Your special possession. I am comforted in knowing You will take good care of me since I am a divine extension of You. I get to operate *from* a place of royal confidence rather than fighting *for* it.

Thank You for designing me to walk with my head held high. **I declare I am clothed in royal robes of strength and dignity. God, I will not be afraid to sing Your praises from a mountain top. I am proud to declare Your wonderful works to everyone who hears me. Thank You for calling me out of darkness into your wonderful light. I am glimmering brightly in the beams of Your light.**

Your *Princess*,

Amen.

DAY 3

Status Update: "@SheisMore I have a pure, sparkling heart and a renewed spirit that reveals my royal identity." #RiseUpPrincess

Create in me a clean heart, O God, and renew a right spirit within me.
Psalm 51:10

My King and Refresher of my Soul,

I thank You so much for alleviating my burdens and the debilitating thoughts that creep into my mind. My heart darkens when I get wrapped up in this world. But every time I come to You and surrender my hurt, anxiety and wrong thinking, You purify my heart once more. You create a clean, sparkling spirit within me.

I am never too much for You because your renewing power has no limits. Thank You for making me weightless and free when I come to You. You are the King and Ruler of my heart and spirit. When I am renewed in You, I feel an unexplainable peace come over me. Suddenly my spiritual eyes are awakened to see how small adversity is through Your eyes.

Thank You for giving me the supernatural gift to be beautifully purified in You so I can live out of my heavenly self. My highest self is unattached from opinions, approval and worldly hardships.

Today, I declare I have a renewed spirit and effervescent heart.

Your *Princess*,

Amen.

DAY 4

Status Update: "@SheisMore I have a new identity through His Perfecting Love!" #RiseUpPrincess

Therefore, if anyone is in Christ, he is a new creation. The old has gone, the new has come.
2 Corinthians 5:17

My King and Perfecting Healer,

*T*hank You that You have made me new. Thank You that my past no longer defines me: the mistakes I made, the hurt I endured, the rejection I faced and the shame I felt shattered me to pieces. I questioned my existence and my worth. You were there the nights I cried my eyes out and begged for You to take me from this world. You waited for me to look up and You reminded me that even though I *made* mistakes, *I* am not a mistake.

Thank You for loving me so much that You have given me the gift of newness in *every* part of me. When I choose Your will, You always give me the exact amount of grace I need to stand strong. My King, I declare right now that the chains of shame, self-hate and emotional wounds are unbound and dead in the past. You have thrown them as far as the east is from the west, evaporated into thin air, nowhere to be retraced.

I get to choose to partake in Your path for me, Your promises and Your plans. I grasp hold of them when I focus on what is ahead and keep my eyes heavenward.

I declare that I will dwell on what is excellent, lovely and pure so I can continue to be transformed and perfected into my Royal Identity. I declare I already see the evidence of newness in my life. I'm so excited for today! Thank You for loving me magnificently through a much needed Identity Adjustment.

Thank you for loving me perfectly with Your Perfecting Love.

Your *P*rincess,

Amen.

DAY 5

Status Update: "@SheisMore
God gave up His only Son so
that I could become His
Daughter." #RiseUpPrincess

*I have been crucified with Christ. It is no
longer I who live, but Christ who lives in me.
And the life I now live in the flesh I live by
faith in the Son of God, who loved me and
gave himself for me.*
Galatians 2:20

My King and Sacrificing Giver,

I often hear of how much You love Your people, but it can be hard for me to fully grasp and understand that Your outrageous love is for me too. You really did give me the ultimate gift by sending Your Perfect Son to die for me.

I can't comprehend how the Prince of Peace came into this fallen world and willingly gave himself up for me. He died just so I could have an intimate relationship with You, the God of the Universe and gain an all-access pass to Your Kingdom. He could have called a thousand angels to save Him from an unspeakable death. But he chose to die so I could have a destiny to be His co-heir in Your Kingdom. Your Son, the Prince of Peace and my Knight in Shining Armor knew Your love for me was worth dying for on the cross.

Just like Christ died in order to give me the Keys to the Kingdom of Heaven, today I die to my ego, my negative thoughts, bad habits, guilt and shame in order to unlock the doors to our Royal Relationship. I want to be all that I am in You, to be everything You say that I am.

I declare I defeat the tactics of the enemy when I walk in my Royal Identity because I am a force for Your mighty Kingdom!

Thank You for Your protection over me as I faithfully continue to show everyone that their citizenship is truly in the Heavenly Realms.

Your *Princess*,

Amen.

D A Y 6

Status Update: "@SheisMore I have put on my new self and I reflect the image of my Creator." #RiseUpPrincess

And have put on the new self, which is being renewed in knowledge after the image of its creator.
Colossians 3:10

My King and Image Perfecter,

*T*hank You for revealing to me that I am made in Your glorious image. My royal design has been weighed down with layers of worldly insecurities and pain. My ego tries to protect me from hurt by shutting people out or repeating the same mistakes. I have realized my ego deceives me in its need to be right by attempting to validate my own negative beliefs with vicious patterns. When my ego agrees with the enemy and says that I don't measure up, I turn to self-sabotage.

My King, today I put off my old self in all of its unhealthy desires and put on my royal tiara to be the princess I truly am. In Your Kingdom, I am Your Princess; I am Royalty. In Your kingdom, I am more than a conqueror and victor. I am not a victim. In Your Throne room, I am capable to win battles before they begin, to take on the world with a passion and a purpose. I am Your confident daughter made perfectly in Your image placed here on this planet to bring hope to a fallen world.

God, thank You for fully equipping me on this journey to ignite my spiritual self when it goes to battle with my flesh.

I declare when my prayers are in alignment with Your will, You always come through on Your promises.

Your *P*rincess,

Amen.

DAY 7

Status Update: "@SheisMore I am renewed in my Royal Identity when I renew my thoughts according to God's truths." #RiseUpPrincess

You were taught, with regard to your former way of life, to put off your old self, which is being corrupted by its deceitful desires; to be made new in the attitude of your minds.
Ephesians 4:22-23

My King and Identity Renewer,

*T*hank You my true citizenship is not of a physical world that I can touch and feel. I was made in a supernatural realm full of glimmering beauty, gold dust and vibrant colors. Heaven is my home and it is where I will return after my mission here is complete. Thank You that heaven is not a far away place up in the sky. It's a place I can tap into around me and inside me when my thoughts aligns with love, beauty and abundance.

The conflict between my old nature and my new nature is a real war. Sometimes I wonder, "*Why does it have to be hard? Why can't I just easily and effortlessly be the Princess I am destined to be all the time?*" But then I remember, our relationship wouldn't be real love if I didn't intentionally choose You back in my weak moments. You have given me the space to make my own decisions and think my own thoughts. Thank You that our relationship grows deeper and more powerfully when I turn away from alluring temptations that only hurt me in the end. As Your Princess, I choose You instead.

Today, I delete the toxic thoughts of my former life, they are just a crippling illusion preventing me from pure happiness and sheer joy. With Your help, I set my heart ablaze with a renewed attitude. **I declare my mind is open to receiving Your noble truths and lovely promises. My new self is positioned to be the revealed, royal woman I am intended to be.** My King, I am on fire for You!

Your *P*rincess,

Amen.

DAY 8

Status Update: "@SheisMore I am saved by grace as a gift, not because of my performance."
#RiseUpPrincess

God saved you by his grace when you believed. And you can't take credit for this; it is a gift from God.
Ephesians 2:8

My King and Abundance of Grace,

*H*ow is it even possible that there is nothing I can do to deserve Your gracious love? It's hard for me to logically grasp because everything around me says perfection earns love. You look at my heart instead. There is no way I can impress You by what I do. I know that when my heart is right, great works will naturally spring forth through me. I realize that the content of my heart and the fruits of my actions are in direct correlation.

My King, thank You for loving me right where I am. Because You Love me so perfectly through my imperfections, I am convicted to turn from my old ways. The old ways that chase boys, material things, parties, alcohol, popularity, accolades, recognition, "likes," and followers on social media. I thought having social status would make me lovable, but I was wrong. Thank You I no longer have to seek approval and acceptance.

Thank You for giving me a new life with bucket loads of gold grace nuggets so I may experience the royal life I am meant to live. Thank You for showering me with the unmerited gift of grace that compels me to love You back in a way I have never loved anyone.

I declare that no thing or person will come between the gift of our Royal Father/Daughter Relationship.

Your *P*rincess,

Amen.

DAY 9

Status Update: "@SheisMore My old habits do not have a place in my life since I live by the Holy Spirit. Now I live a royal lifestyle. #RiseUpPrincess

And Peter said to them, "Repent and be baptized every one of you in the name of Jesus Christ for the forgiveness of your sins, and you will receive the gift of the Holy Spirit.
Acts 2:38

My King and Gentle Forgiver,

*T*hank You for stretching Your arms out to me and choosing me first. Thank You that You knew me in the heavens before I was formed in my mother's womb. I am so grateful that when I chose you back, not only was I set free from all of my burdens and past mistakes, I was also given a miraculous and eternal gift. I don't know how I ever lived without the gift of the Holy Spirit in my life.

When I agree with the Holy Spirit every day, I experience a super-charged life. I am connected to the ebb and flow of the Source of Life, the Creator of beauty, and the Builder of all things lovely and good.

Today, I declare that the flame of the Holy Spirit expands to every inch of my heart, soul, mind and body. Thank You that your Spirit enables me to do all things in alignment with Your good and perfect will. My King, I receive Your powerful Spirit today and I declare that I will live my royal life with purpose and passion. After all, I am…

Your *P*rincess,

Amen.

DAY 10

Status Update: "@SheisMore I create my present and my future because my past is powerless in defining me. #RiseUpPrincess

For behold, I create new heavens and a new earth, and the former things shall not be remembered or come into mind.
Isaiah 65:17

My King and New Reality Giver,

*Y*ou are an incredibly good God! There have been crazy things that have hurt me in the past. I have made mistakes and hurt my family and others who care about me. I have lived in fear and made decisions out of fear. God, I know that the opposite of fear is perfect love, and You are my Perfect Love.

Thank You for the gift of renewal You offer me every day. Thank You that when I received You as the King of my life, I became a new creation. Because of Your Spirit that lives within me, I am empowered to set my thoughts on enjoying the present and I can dream about my future. I don't have to be trapped in the memory of my past any longer. When my thoughts are focused on heavenly things, I can create a new reality for myself…a royal reality.

As Your princess, I declare that I have a royal life with royal capabilities, beliefs and possibilities. I am fully capable of releasing every former memory that does not serve me. Instead, I meditate on the new and beautiful memories I intend to create through You.

Your *P*rincess,

Amen.

DAY 11

Status Update: "@SheisMore My past is behind me and now I live in His royal light."
#RiseUpPrincess

He has delivered us from the domain of darkness and transferred us to the kingdom of his beloved Son.
Colossians 1:13

My King and Deliverer from Darkness,

*Y*ou have transferred me into Your dazzling Light by delivering me from dark places. There were seasons I thought I would never come out of my depression. Even in this very moment, as I choose to spend time with You, I feel Your warmth washing my pain away. I immediately feel lighter when I fill my mind and heart with the Sword of your Word.

God, it can be so hard to keep my eyes on You. It's so hard to believe that You actually have great plans for me when it seems like I am forgotten or left behind. I know feelings can be deceiving and I believe You are always working behind the scenes for my good. I will not live by what I feel, I will live by what I know. I do not have to *feel* confident in order to *be* confident. The only solid truth I know is what You have promised me.

I declare I have already been delivered from the domain of darkness and You transferred me into Your kingdom that reigns. Today, I release all feelings of darkness and I receive the beauty of Your kingdom in exchange. Through Your Son, I declare I am radiant as the shining sun from the inside out.

Your *Princess*,

Amen.

35

DAY 12

Status Update: "@SheisMore I have
been set free from the burden of
performance and perfection."
#RiseUpPrincess

*For sin will have no dominion over you, since
you are not under law but under grace.*
Romans 6:14

My King,

I am speechless today. I'm feeling so grateful and in awe of You. Your overwhelming love and grace is so mysterious and unfathomable to me. You set me free every day from the chains that attempt to shackle me in the shame from my past. It is so easy for me to be mean to myself, to tell myself that I am unworthy of the freedom to enjoy my royal identity.

Today God, I say *NO* to shame, *NO* to negative self-talk and *YES* to freedom. Your Word says no sin or injustice has dominion over me. As Your daughter, I am under /Your exceeding and abundant grace. I ask for forgiveness and turn away from my old behavior that is unfit for a Royal Princess. Thank You, my sweet King for loving me to the point that brings me to my knees.

I declare I am royalty because I live freely and fearlessly. The dominion of sin has been removed from my path and the crown of life awaits me.

Your *Princess*,

Amen.

DAY 13

Status Update: "@SheisMore My Father is the King of the Universe. That makes me His princess."
#RiseUpPrincess

Who would not fear you, O King of nations? That title belongs to you alone! Among all the wise people of the earth and in all the kingdoms of the world, there is no one like you.
Jeremiah 10:7

My King of the Universe,

I am so blessed to call You my Father, my King, my Creator, my Maker, my Protector and my Comforter and all the countless beautiful names You are to me. I know people worship gods from different religions and philosophies. I feel so blessed and lucky that I get to call the One and Only King of Kingdoms of the World my Father.

You are the only One that this title will ever belong to. I can not even fathom that You would choose me first and I am so joyful I have the opportunity to choose You every day. You have transformed my heart, my identity and my life. There is no other like You.

Among the celebrities, the heroes, the politicians, philosophers, Nobel Peace Prize winners and all the influencers of the world, I will never idolize a person's greatness before Your greatness.

I get to be the King's Daughter, therefore I am infused with the Royal blood to lead by my example. As Your Princess, I will expand Your Kingdom to all ends of the earth.

Your *Princess*,

Amen.

DAY 14

Status Update: "@SheisMore I belong to the King who gives me a Royal Identity in Christ." #RiseUpPrincess

I belong to my beloved, and his desire is for me.
Song of Solomon 7:10

My King and One to Whom I belong,

*T*hank You that I am Yours. I am not my own or anyone else's. I belong to You. No one is allowed to treat me beneath Your royal approval. Your royal standards fall on every aspect of my life, including relationships with family, friends and romantic interests.

I belong to You and Your desire is for *all* of me: my heart, my soul, my mind and my body. Every part of me is designed to praise and honor the good work of Your hands. My beloved, You cherish every part of me and adore me in a way that transforms me to the core. My heart melts in Your presence because I am reminded how precious I am to You.

My beloved God, I declare that I am Yours and You are mine. You call out for me when I wander off and You console me with gentle whispers when I cry. I declare that your loving desire always brings me back to the Throne.

Your *Princess*,

Amen.

DAY 15

Status Update: "@SheisMore My King sees my beauty in my ugly moments." #RiseUpPrincess

How beautiful you are, my darling! Oh, how beautiful! Your eyes are doves.
Song of Solomon 1:15

My King and my Love,

*M*y heart skips a beat when You call me darling. When I feel unworthy of Your affection, it is hard to receive Your love. In my weakness I have dark thoughts, I get angry and say things that hurt people. I feel so guilty about it. No matter how I feel or what I do, You still see my beauty. You may not like what I do, but that doesn't change your unfailing love for me.

You say that my eyes are like doves. Doves are symbolic of peace and Your Presence. There is no other way to describe me that could be more powerful and lovely. In my moments of self-doubt, I surrender my defenses and trust that you still call me *darling* and *beautiful*. I am symbolic of Your peace and Your Presence.

I declare that my eyes are beautiful because they see the beauty in others, and bring beauty to broken places. I declare that I have the royal vision to see myself as beautiful as You see me.

Your *P*rincess,

Amen.

DAY 16

Status Update: "@SheisMore I am a
woman of invaluable worth."
#RiseUpPrincess

Her worth is far more precious than rubies.
Proverbs 3:15

My King and Divine Gemologist,

I question my meaning, my value, and my worth. I feel unimportant and small. It seems that everyone around me knows their purpose and they seem so confident. I feel intimated by groups of people, like I don't belong. Anxiety wells up inside me when I walk into parties or rooms of people.

In my life, I have settled for treatment below my dignity because I thought it was the only way someone would stay. I have settled and compromised my morals in exchange for affection from a boy. I wanted so bad for him to love me that I did anything to make him stay. I have sold out on my dreams in exchange for the comfort of sitting on the sidelines.

Today, I turn back to You and I turn away from the fear that cripples my divine worth. I release my fear of people, rejection and failure. I throw all of my insecurities and false beliefs onto You. The lies I have believed are not from You, they are from this broken world. Your over-riding truth says my value is far more precious than rubies and rare jewels.

God, I cast out the debilitating lies that have prevented an epic life and true love. Your Word says I am immeasurably more worthy than rare gems and precious stones.

I declare that Your opinion is the only one that matters. I am more than enough and worthy of a life that inspires others.

Your *Princess*,

Amen.

DAY 17

Status Update: "@SheisMore I am beautifully flawless in the eyes of The Only One who matters!" #RiseUpPrincess

You are altogether beautiful, my darling; there is no flaw in you.
Song of Solomon 4:7

My King and Beauty Seer,

I praise You today for making me so flawlessly beautiful! You romance my heart so intimately with Your sweet promises and truth. You are incomparable to any guy whose selfish motives are masked in sweet charm and flattery. My Father, You shower me with refreshing, exuberating words because they are the Truth.

Thank You for desiring me to see the magnitude of my flawless beauty. You imagined me from your Throne room. My eyes, my hair, my heart, my arms, my legs, my hands, my feet and especially my spirit are absolutely and entirely exquisite. **God, I declare that when I look in the mirror, I see the Princess you destined me to be.**

If there is any celebrity whose beauty I admire, You are infinitely more enamored by me. Open my spiritual eyes to see that there is no flaw in me. **When I believe I am a flawless beauty, I treat myself with flawless kindness. I declare that I am altogether beautiful, my King. I will twirl and celebrate my beautiful, feminine design today.**

Your *Princess*,

Amen.

DAY 18

Status Update: "@SheisMore My spirit is reborn and empowered by the royal Spirit of God."
#RiseUpPrincess

Jesus answered, *"Very truly I tell you, no one can enter the kingdom of God unless they are born of water and the Spirit. Flesh gives birth to flesh, but the Spirit gives birth to spirit."*
John 3:3-6

My King and Renewer of Life,

*T*hank You for giving me the gift to have full access to your magical and wondrous kingdom from right where I am. It's wondrous that I can be sitting in my room and still taste heaven's glory. As Your daughter, I am entrusted to preview the Heavenly City that is to come. I get to taste, see, hear, and feel it every day because my spirit and soul have been born again in You.

Thank You for forming me in my mother's womb and choosing the perfect woman to give birth to me. Thank You for making me wonderful in the flesh by specifically appointing my mother and father. I know Your reasons are always perfect even when my parent's aren't. Now that I have been born again by the power of Your Holy Spirit, I have been catapulted to new dimensions of potential and greatness through You.

Thank You for birthing Your Spirit within me. I magnify Your Presence by agreeing with what you say about my Royal Identity.

As your daughter, I walk in the fruits of the Holy Spirit which are love, joy, peace, patience, kindness, goodness, self-discipline and faith. When I choose these qualities over my old nature, I am spiritually promoted to explosive levels!

Your *P*rincess,

Amen.

DAY 19

Status Update: @SheisMore I emulate
Godly character because that is how I
was created." #RiseUpPrincess

And to put on the new self, created to be like
God in true righteousness and holiness.
Ephesians 4:24

My King and One who makes me Holy,

You made me in Your image! I am in pure awe when I fathom the idea that I am not a sinner. I am pure and holy because that is how You made me! Right now, I repent of the lie that I am a sinner. Only the enemy wants me to believe that so he can cause me to stumble through my own self-talk and wrong beliefs.

Thank You so much that I am holy, godly and righteous in the way I talk, in the way I treat people and in the decisions I make, especially when no one else is looking. You are so sweet, My King. As Your daughter, I am a representation of You.

I declare that I am your mirror image. When people see me, they will see Your perfect love illuminating through my eyes and smile. I reveal Love everywhere I go and my love tank is refilled in my alone time with You.

Your Princess,

Amen.

DAY 20

Status Update: "@SheisMore I glorify my body because it was bought with an invaluable price." #RiseUpPrincess

For you were bought with a price. So glorify God in your body.
1 Corinthians 6:20

My King,

*T*hank You for loving me so much that You didn't leave me to myself. You thought of everything. You knew I would have dark urges to hurt myself when I felt unwanted and weak. My body is not mine to neglect or sabotage through detrimental diets, substance abuse or self-harm. You foresaw my false belief that self-inflicted physical harm was my only emotional release. You made my body Your temple!

My Maker, I am sorry for hurting myself. I am sorry for neglecting my well-being. I repent of my harmful behavior today and commit to treasuring my body instead with healthy choices. I can't fulfill my royal identity without taking care of the vessel through which Your presence flows. When I am hurt, I will turn to prayer and safe friendships for release instead of self-sabotage.

God, thank You for making my body exactly what it is supposed to be. I praise You for imagining and crafting my divine design. You do not make mistakes and I embrace the way in which You crafted me to be unique.

I declare my body is a walking autobiography. I wear the way I feel about myself on the outside. Today I declare that I love myself and my flawless, feminine design.

Your *P*rincess,

Amen.

she *Reveals*

her true identity

Congratulations! Your 20 Day *She Reveals* journey is complete! Seal your commitment in the contract below:

I, _____, am committed to unveiling the mask I thought was protecting me. I am committed to forgetting the past and believing the good plans God has for my future. I am committed to being authentic in the royal identity God made me to be.

When I seek approval from God, approval from the right people will naturally come. I am committed to honoring my body and seeing myself as a priceless treasure. Today, I remove the mask of lies, insecurities and my false self-image and replace it with the crown of Truth.

Today, My royal identity is *Revealed.*

she

Radiates

her beauty and light

DAY 21

Status Update: "@SheisMore I radiate light wherever I go." #RiseUpPrincess

You are the light of the world. A town built on a hill cannot be hidden.
Matthew 5:14

My King and Radiance Instiller,

You have breathed Your light into me so I would be the light of the world! Because I am Your daughter, I am born to shine. You have entrusted me to be like a city on a hilltop. I will no longer sink in the background or stand quietly on the sidelines.

Thank You for giving me the ability to shine bright when I step out in courage and take leaps of faith. It is easy to allow the boldness of others to intimidate me, but thank You for reminding me that You are the Light in me and no one has the authority to darken it. A spirit of timidity is not from You. Instead, You have given me a spirit of boldness and of sound mind. Father, thank You for entrusting me with Your blessings when I trust in You.

I declare that I will be a light for Your city. You created me, therefore I am not meant to be hidden. I am meant to be seen and I am designed to be a leader.

Your *Princess*,

Amen.

DAY 22

Status Update: "@SheisMore I
shine like a firework in the night."
#RiseUpPrincess

*Then you will shine among them like stars in
the sky.*
Philippians 2:15

My King and Star Breather,

I am made to burst with Your divine light when I step out into the world today. I already feel You glimmering vibrantly inside of me because my joy is overflowing. Thank You that I don't have to dull my sparkle so other people feel comfortable. I don't have to worry about being a target of jealousy because You say that You always have my back. You are my Defender so I have nothing to fear.

Thank You God for infusing my soul with the empowering flame of Your Spirit. I will release love on every person I meet today not because they have been nice to me, but because they are Your children. I know that my kindness will ultimately soften their soul, if not towards me, then towards someone else.

I declare that as Your Princess, I will melt hearts and inspire others with Your Love, especially to the forgotten, broken and lonely.

Your *Princess*,

Amen.

DAY 23

Status Update: "@SheisMore I am a daughter of Light." #RiseUpPrincess

You are all children of the light and children of the day. We do not belong to the night or to the darkness.
1 Thessalonians 5:5

My King and Light Maker,

*T*hank You for wrapping me in a robe of brightness. There are days that different faces of the dark side confront me. They are faces of depression, shame, insecurity and temptation trying to creep in. In my weakness, it seems it would be easier to let them win, but I do not belong to them! They are children of darkness and I am *Your Daughter of Light.*

Thank You for the gift of spiritual discernment so I can easily detect when darkness attempts to break into my Light Realm. I am a force for good and that makes me a target to the enemy, but I am a princess who causes the enemy to shrink back in defeat. My weapons of laughter, prayer and singing praise always win. I declare that darkness will never have a place over me.

You have already taken the keys back from the enemy and restored Your dominion with light, so I walk in truth and identity. My radiant joy will not be stolen by a force that has been defeated once and for all by Jesus. I declare I am a princess of light.

Your *P*rincess,

Amen.

DAY 24

Status Update: "@SheisMore I
am a vessel of Divine Light."
#RiseUpPrincess

*For God, who said, "Let light shine out of
darkness," made his light shine in our hearts
to give us the light of the knowledge of God's
glory displayed in the face of Christ.*
2 Corinthians 4:6

My King and Penetrator of Darkness,

*T*hank You for beaming a light into my heart to reveal Your love. My spiritual eyes are sharpened to see Your consuming love displayed through Christ. Thank You for giving me the spiritual wisdom and maturity to recognize You as my King so I don't have to waste time seeking meaningless things.

Thank You for commissioning me to be a transformer. When I am bold in calling out the beauty in others, Your revealing light transforms shattered hearts into magnificent mosaics of inspiring testimonies. Just as the sunlight beams through a stained glass window, my light will be a healing agent to the hurt and broken.

Thank You for strengthening me to stand up for everything lovely, noble and true, especially when I am pressured to compromise my morals and values. Thank You for enabling me to be strong in the decisions I make. I am a light among my peers, family and especially among those who are mean to me.

I declare that others will be led to the knowledge of Your glory displayed through the light of my actions, words and decisions.

Your *P*rincess,

Amen.

DAY 25

Status Update: "@SheisMore I wear a beautiful crown on my head, one that no one can ever take away." #RiseUpPrincess

In that day the LORD Almighty will be a glorious crown, a beautiful wreath for the remnant of his people.
Isaiah 28:5

My King and Crowning Beauty,

*T*hank You for Your majestic covering wherever I walk. Whether I am in shadows of fear or threatened by my enemies, I am covered and safe in Your wings. You are a beautiful wreath that adorns my head so people know I am Yours without even saying a word.

They see I am loved and I am protected. The arrows of hurtful words and unjust actions are quickly dissipated by Your shield. My enemies see their attempts fail because I do not give them power by agreeing with emotional defeat. I remain resilient because Your glorious crown empowers me. I wear my crown in realms of influence by representing steadfast peace, compassion and strength. You promise that my enemies will soon repent and be convicted by Your fiery love emanating through me.

I declare that on that day, You will be the glorious crown, the beautiful adorning crown that everyone sees. Thank You for the fresh infilling of fire that You are igniting inside of me right now. I am radiant in beauty when I abide in You.

Your *P*rincess,

Amen.

DAY 26

Status Update: "@SheisMore I sparkle like a royal jewel in God's land, which is all of the world." #RiseUpPrincess

The LORD their God will save his people on that day as a shepherd saves his flock. They will sparkle in his land like jewels in a crown.
Zechariah 9:16

My King and Crowning Jewel,

*Y*ou have anointed me to sparkle like jewels in a crown. Father, today I need a fresh infilling of Your radiant essence. I feel weighted down with toxic thoughts swirling in my head. I feel the enemy playing on my insecurities. My sparkle has dulled and I feel like I'm slowly drowning.

Thank You for lifting me out of the pit this moment, my King! I am Your princess and I am crying out to You in desperation. Please, save me from myself. Save me from this downward spiral of obscure thoughts that are clouding Your precious truths. Thank You for being my Shepherd who comes looking for me when I lose my way. You care about me as Your one and only.

God, I surrender fighting this battle on my own right now. I lay down the people and things I have sought to fill my emptiness. When I am apart from You, I lose access to pure and complete joy. Thank You for being quick to rescue me and quick to restore me.

Today, I will delete all of my negative thoughts and re-align my mind with the hope that is in Christ. I declare I have reclaimed my sparkle and I radiate like the jewels in your crown wherever I go.

Your *P*rincess,

Amen.

DAY 27

Status Update: "@SheisMore God chose me before He even formed the world and blessed me with every spiritual blessing in the heavens." #RiseUpPrincess

Blessed be the God and Father of our Lord Jesus Christ, who has blessed us in Christ with every spiritual blessing in the heavenly places, even as he chose us in him before the foundation of the world, that we should be holy and blameless before him.
Ephesians 1:3-4

My King and my One Chooser,

*B*efore You formed the foundation of the world, You formed the idea of me. I am in awe and mesmerized that You uniquely created me. I rise up because I have access to every spiritual blessing in the heavenly places. I admit it is challenging to fully comprehend the spiritual power I carry when the world has pushed me down so many times. People let me down, my dreams have been crushed and my heart has been shattered.

I know when I match my thoughts with Your thoughts, I grow stronger in operating out of my spiritual blessings.

I declare I have been chosen for purity and a blameless reputation. I delete any memory, thought or person that isn't beneficial to me and replace it with the beauty of Your absolute truth. Your Truth says I am blameless when I choose joy, peace, faith and hope to reign in my life instead of circumstances. I can function out of the same spiritual power that rose Jesus from the dead.

God, thank You for Your purifying love that makes me blameless and radiant.

Your *P*rincess,

Amen.

DAY 28

Status Update: "@SheisMore I am God's treasured and precious possession out of everyone on the face of the earth." #RiseUpPrincess

For you are a people holy to the Lord your God, and the Lord has chosen you to be a people for his treasured possession, out of all the peoples who are on the face of the earth.
Deuteronomy 14:2

My King and my Heart Treasurer,

*Y*ou say that I am holy to You. You say that I am chosen to be treasured out of everyone else on the face of the earth. Holiness means to be *set apart* specifically for You and Your Kingdom. Today, I choose to see myself the way You see me. I am tired of being my own enemy. I choose to see my heart, mind and actions through the lens of a royal princess. If You say that I have been set apart for You and to be Your treasure, then I have been empowered for royalty.

When I choose to carry myself as a treasure, You will strengthen me to do so. It might not feel natural at first because of my old habits. Each time I defy my flesh and honor my royal identity, it becomes a little easier to treat myself as a rare jewel.

Today, I will value myself as the treasure that I am. I will think like a treasure, act like a treasure and speak like a treasure. Even if I don't feel like I am chosen and important at first, I know that what I feel isn't important. I declare I will set my mind on Your truth that always prevails and sets me free.

Your *P*rincess,

Amen.

DAY 29

Status Update: "@SheisMore I am safe and secure when I keep my heart set on My King." #RiseUpPrincess

I have set the Lord always before me; because he is at my right hand, I shall not be shaken. Therefore my heart is glad, and my whole being rejoices; my flesh also dwells secure. For you will not abandon my soul to Sheol, or let your holy one see corruption. You make known to me the path of life; in your presence there is fullness of joy; at your right hand are pleasures forevermore.
Psalm 16:8-11

My King and My Safety,

I set my sight on You and make You a priority today and everyday. When I keep You front and center, I am never shaken. Not only is my spirit safe and secure in the heavens, my physical self is too. I will not be shaken by my enemies, people who hurt me, breakups or rejection. Nothing has the power to tear me down because You have already crushed the head of the enemy and all the authorities of the dark world.

Thank You God for protecting me, for being my rock and safety. Thank You for covering my heart with Your unbreakable shield in order to elevate me to new levels. Because I am your Holy One, I am protected from any attempted corruption to my destiny and the beautiful plans You have in store. You clearly highlight the path that leads to life, abundance and the fullness of my royal identity.

When I praise Your name and spend time in song, intimacy and silence with You, I experience an indescribable joy.

I declare by abiding in You, Your word and promises, I can be who You say I am and have what you say I have. In You, the pleasures I experience are infinite and limitless. Thank You for being the most awesome Father I could ever ask for.

Your *Princess*,

Amen.

DAY 30

Status Update: "@SheisMore I make decisions for God's approval, therefore I remain radiant in my strength." #RiseUpPrincess

For am I now seeking the approval of man, or of God? Or am I trying to please man? If I were still trying to please man, I would not be a servant of Christ.
Galatians 1:10

My King and my True Approver,

*W*hen I try to please people, I am distracted from my Kingdom purpose. I've realized it is impossible to please everyone. No matter what I do for some people, it will never be enough. Sometimes I exhaust myself by running in a million directions, trying to get everyone to like me by pouring out all that I have.

Thank You for giving me the wisdom to understand that ten percent of people will never like me, no matter how much I give or accommodate them. My King, now I understand why I am called to please *You,* to honor and seek approval in *Your* eyes first and foremost. You have one set of pure standards and I can live in peace as long as I am pleasing You.

I surrender every relationship to You that isn't pleasing in Your sight. I surrender my desire to be approved by people. **When I live to honor You, the right approval will eventually come from the right people. I declare that when I entrust the results in Your hands, I will experience the gift of freedom.**

Your *P*rincess,

Amen.

DAY 31

Status Update: "@SheisMore I am purified of all strongholds and empowered to live a Kingdom life." #RiseUpPrincess

But if it is by the Spirit of God that I cast out demons, then the kingdom of God has come upon you.
Matthew 12:28

My King and my Strength,

*T*hank You for designing me to radiate from the inside-out. I don't stand out because of the clothes or jewelry I wear, the make-up I use or how often I exercise. I am glowing because Your Kingdom is upon me. All the beautiful fruits of the spirit are within me. It's something so powerful, infinite and expansive that it can not be taken away. People might try to muffle my enthusiasm because they don't understand it, but no one has the authority to make a negative impact on me unless I agree with them.

Only You have the authority to define my worth and unique beauty. Today, I agree Your Kingdom has come upon me and I have access to all its riches, light and goodness. Your kingdom is like a refreshing stream of water running through my soul. Because Your glorious spirit is within me, I declare that any demonic stronghold is cast out of me right now in Jesus name.

Thank You God that I am Royalty. Thank You that I carry Your DNA because I am an expression of You. I declare that I am Your warrior princess that brings a message of hope wherever I go.

Your *P*rincess,

Amen.

DAY 32

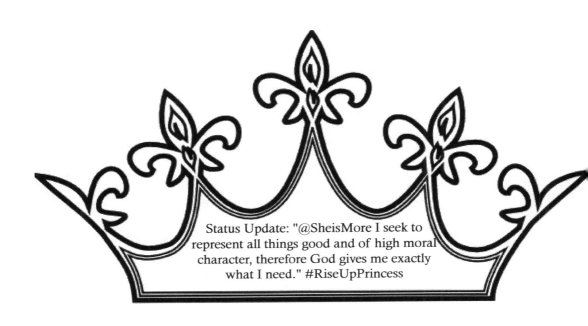

Status Update: "@SheisMore I seek to represent all things good and of high moral character, therefore God gives me exactly what I need." #RiseUpPrincess

Seek first the Kingdom of God above all else and live righteously, and he will give you everything you need.
Matthew 6:33

My King,

*S*ociety is driven by wealth, status and success. I am often faced with difficult decisions to choose between two good things. It would be so easy to choose the one that is immediately gratifying, especially financially. The recognition or praise I could get from certain opportunities in the spotlight are so tempting. I feel a pressure to strive and hustle in order to succeed and be seen.

Thank You God for alleviating that stress and burden. You have made success and provision an easy formula to live by. You say that when I seek first the kingdom of God and live with integrity, You will give me everything I need.

As Your Princess, I declare that I will choose the right thing instead of the easy thing. I will honor You when I stand up for what is right and in return will receive exactly what I need. I radiate light through my decisions that reflect love, joy, peace, righteousness, self-discipline, kindness and high moral character. As I abide in the kingdom, all the glory and goodness of the kingdom will abide in me.

Your *P*rincess,

Amen.

DAY 33

Status Update: "@SheisMore I am imprinted on the heart of God and His love sets my heart ablaze." #RiseUpPrincess

Set me as a seal upon your heart, as a seal upon your arm, for love is strong as death, jealousy is fierce as the grave. Its flashes are flashes of fire, the very flame of the Lord.
Song of Solomon 8:7

My King and Fierce Lover,

$\mathcal{I}$ have struggled with feeling loved, wanted and accepted. It often led to harmful, unhealthy patterns that almost destroyed me. I have tried to fill my lack of self-love with things like alcohol, drugs, adrenaline rushes, over-exercising, extreme dieting, cutting, sex or over-spending. It was hard for me to understand that the God of the Universe actually loves *me*, apart from everyone else. You have set me as a seal upon Your heart and a permanent impression on Your arm because I am that important to You.

I often feel like love is for other people and I am not worthy of having an epic love story. I wonder if I would have been a good enough child, maybe I would've seen what real love looks like. But, *You* are the most divine romance and intimacy I could have ever hoped for or dreamed to experience. I am sorry for placing my search for perfect love in people.

Today, I break down the walls I believed were protecting me and I open my heart to receive Your rejuvenating love. You are a God who loves *me* deeply and truly. You love the pain, the joy, the good and the broken parts of me. Nothing surprises You or stops Your healing embrace. Thank You God for having a divine jealously so fierce that You will vindicate anyone who wrongs me. Your love for me is as strong as death. Today, I receive the fire of Your Holy Spirit that sets my heart ablaze.

Your $\mathcal{P}$rincess,

Amen.

DAY 34

Status Update: "@SheisMore I am celebrated with a banner of love waving over me." #RiseUpPrincess

He brought me to the banqueting house, and his banner over me was love.
Song of Solomon 2:1-17

My King and Love Celebrator,

I am radiant basking in Your celebratory love over me today. You say that there is a love banner over me every time I come into Your Presence. I look back on my life and realize You were there in all those heartbreaking moments and in all the amazing moments. You have never left my side. You have been gently waiting for me to turn my eyes to You, to acknowledge your presence and power.

That realization wrecks my heart. It wrecks me because I thought I had to find You. I thought you had left me. The truth is, You were there all along. Through every tear, every disappointment and every heartbreak. How are You so faithful? So loving? So true? From this moment, I will keep my gaze locked on Yours. You have shown me what true love is by laying down Your life in order for me to have a better one. You have done this for me. You created me in the heavens before I was born and sent me to Earth with a divine purpose. You loved me so much that You gave me the freewill to choose You back and love You in return.

God, no glittering treasure can compete with the fire I feel when I am in Your presence, wrapped in Your arms. My life is full when I love You with my whole heart, mind and soul because it is then that I can experience Your overwhelming love for me. Thank You My King for empowering me.

I declare that I love You with my whole heart, my whole mind and my whole soul. Your banner over me is love and I have been transformed into royalty.

Your *Princess*,

Amen.

DAY 35

Status Update: "@SheisMore My
God is my beloved and my heart is
safe in His hands."
#RiseUpPrincess

*My beloved is mine, and I am his; he grazes
among the lilies.*
Song of Solomon 2:16

My King and my Beloved,

Today, I am comforted with the peace in knowing I am Yours and You are mine. I can have alone time with You whenever I make time. You are not too busy for me and my worries are never too small for You to care about. If something matters to me, it matters to You.

Thank You God for always being there with a listening, compassionate ear the moment I call out for You. Thank You for cradling my heart in Your hands. My heart had aching cracks, but You restored my wounds back to wholeness. You are my beloved and I entrust my heart to You alone. Thank You for reminding me that I am Your Princess with a still, small voice and the comforting sensation that runs through me when I cry.

I never have to perform for Your attention or approval. You always see me through eyes of adoration no matter what I look like or how I feel. I love soaking in the wonder of Your love. I wish I had all the hours in the day and night to bask in Your Spirit.

Today, I declare I will set my imagination on our time together, among lilies in a field. You are my beloved and I am Yours.

Your Princess,

Amen.

DAY 36

Status Update: "@SheisMore I honor my body because it hosts the Presence of God." #RiseUpPrincess

Or do you not know that your body is a temple of the Holy Spirit within you, whom you have from God? You are not your own, for you were bought with a price. So glorify God in your body.
1 Corinthians 6:19-20

My King and Sacred Presence,

Often times, I treat my body below my royal dignity when I doubt my self-worth. But God, You say that I am Your chosen Princess. You have entrusted me to host the gift of Your Holy Spirit. There is nothing that can reiterate my royal worth more than that.

My King, thank You for creating my body to exemplify a walk of purity, self-respect and honor. I am sorry for seeking validation through sexual acts or destructive health habits. I repent of the lie that sex ever made a man love a woman.

My God, even when I struggle with feeling unworthy, I declare that the Perfect Love I have in You is enough. My body belongs to You, therefore I will honor myself even when I have urges to give myself away to someone who doesn't deserve me. Today, I declare that I am more than enough, more than worthy of loving my body. When I hold my body in high regard, I am glorifying Your handiwork.

Your Princess,

Amen.

DAY 37

Status Update: "@SheisMore I am a crown of beauty in the Lord's hands." #RiseUpPrincess

You shall be a crown of beauty in the hand of the Lord, a royal diadem in the hand of your God.
Isaiah 62:3

My King and Royal Designer,

*T*hank You for designing me to represent Your beauty and royalty when I walk in Your truth. I am not distracted by unrealistic images of photo-shopped models and celebrities. In Your majestic eyes, I am Your crowning jewel, Your crown of beauty.

Thank You for creating me as an ambassador of Your love and passion for beauty. Your passion for beauty is clear when I am awestruck by the vibrant colors of the flowers and the breathtaking brushstrokes in your sunsets. If You have made the flowers and the sunsets this lovely, how much more lovely did you make me?

Eve was the grand finale of your Creation. She was the crowning touch. She represented Your expression of feminine and relational beauty. As her descendant, You have also placed me as the crowning touch of every beautiful thing. Thank You that I am empowered to feel, live and act as a royal princess.

I declare when I follow Your guidance, You supernaturally empower me to do things I couldn't do on my own. I'm like a royal diadem in Your hands. I declare I am destined to radiate like a crown of beauty.

Your *P*rincess,

Amen.

DAY 38

Status Update: "@SheisMore I will rise up in love and see my true beauty today because that is my divine calling." #RiseUpPrincess

My beloved speaks and says to me: **"Arise, my love, my beautiful one**, *and come away, for behold, the winter is past; the rain is over and gone. The flowers appear on the earth, the time of singing has come, and the voice of the turtledove is heard in our land. The fig tree ripens its figs, and the vines are in blossom; they give forth fragrance.* **Arise, my love, my beautiful one,** *and come away."*
Song of Solomon 1:10-13

My King and Heavenly Fragrance,

*I*n You, my old nature is gone and You have transformed me into Royalty. I am Your daughter, therefore the emotional scars and wounding inflicted on Earth have been wiped away. It doesn't matter what my past looks like or how bad the trials are, You are my Heavenly Father, the One who has never left my side.

I discovered You the moment I reached out for You and I am never letting go. You cleanse me with the water of your words and call me to rise up. You call me Your beautiful one and beckon me to come into The Kingdom. When I stepped into my royal identity, my world melted from a rainy winter into a flowery spring. My dreams and faith have strengthened and my confidence is flourishing. Now, my presence carries a heavenly fragrance everywhere I go because I have blossomed in divine beauty and love.

I declare that I will continue to rise up in beauty and love because the rain is over and gone. Spring has come, I am in full bloom and emanate a royal essence that inspires confidence in others.

Your *P*rincess,

Amen.

DAY 39

Status Update: "@SheisMore My beauty is
unfading because I have a gentle spirit which
is invaluable in God's eyes."
#RiseUpPrincess

*Your beauty should not come from outward
adornment, such as elaborate hairstyles and the
wearing of gold jewelry or fine clothes. Rather, it
should be that of your inner self, the unfading
beauty of a gentle and quiet spirit, which is of great
worth in God's sight.*
1 Peter 3:3-4

My King and Beautifer,

*T*hank You that I do not need to be preoccupied with creams, serums and treatments to waste my precious time trying to maintain youthfulness or perfect skin. Thank You God that I am more than my outward appearance, and I am confident in my divine physical design. Thank You for carefully crafting me to be more than meets the eye.

I have no need to define my worth through expensive haircuts, dazzling jewelry or designer brands. Since I have been stamped with Your approval, I do not need to impress people with a perception of social status and beauty.

Thank You, my King, that I am even more stunning on the inside than my external beauty could ever be because my spirit is gentle and quiet. My inner spirit is beautifully unfading and highly valued by You, My Maker.

I declare that since I am Your precious daughter, I am an example of true beauty through radiating your Light with unwavering confidence today.

Your *P*rincess,

Amen.

DAY 40

Status Update: "@SheisMore God protects me in the shadow of His wings because I am His daughter."
#RiseUpPrincess

Keep me as the apple of your eye; hide me in the shadow of your wings.
Psalm 17:8

My King and Wing-Shadower,

*T*hank You for making me to be an expression of Your perfect image. My prayer is to be transformed to look more like You every day. When people see me, I want them to see You. I want to hear people say, "Like Father, like daughter." God, keep me as the apple of Your eye. Don't let me fall into depression or despair.

Thank You for drawing me close to You when I start to waver in my weakness. Thank You for hiding me in the shadow of Your wings when the circumstances and enemies in my life entrench me in their claws. Thank You for being my refuge, my safe haven. All I have to do is cry out and You dispatch a fleet of angels to surround me.

I declare that even in the midst of chaos, I will operate out of the rest found in the shadow of Your wings. You keep me as the apple of your eye, especially in moments of chaos or confusion. I declare that the radiant hope of Christ will be seen through me.

Your *P*rincess,

Amen.

she Radiates
her beauty and light

Congratulations Princess! Your 20 Day *She Radiates* journey is complete! Seal your new radiance in the contract below:

I, _____, am committed to radiating inner beauty and confidence everywhere I go. I am committed to only speaking kind words about myself that honor God's craftsmanship. I will love and nurture my heart, mind and body by respecting myself, setting healthy boundaries and dwelling on divine truths.

I am committed to radiating the love of God and to stepping up to be the light of the world. God has made me to shine hope and truth like a city on a hilltop. I fully intend to stay in the light so I can be the light for others. I am committed to seeing the beauty in myself so I can easily see the divine beauty in others.

I wear a crown of favor and illuminate atmospheres with my Godly confidence and joy.

My royal identity is *Radiant.*

she

Reigns

with her royal purpose

DAY 41

Status Update: "@SheisMore I live a passionate, disciplined and focused life not *for* earthly accolades, but *because* of the everlasting crown I have inherited." #RiseUpPrincess

Everyone who competes in the games goes into strict training. They do it to get a crown that will not last, but we do it to get a crown that will last forever.
1 Corinthians 9:25

My King and Coronator,

I am in strict training because I have inherited the Crown of Life. I see people all around me competing for the sake of recognition, accolades and trophies. I know the high points of worldly winnings are short-lived and unfulfilling. They have left me empty because I was seeking identity through accomplishments rather than *accomplishing through identity*.

When my self-worth is rooted in people, I am constantly wavering and unstable in my confidence. I know people whose happiness and identity tosses to and fro, always dependent on the feedback from the world. Their eyes are empty and wandering. I want so much to reveal the wholeness and joy that comes from the Only Crown of Approval.

I declare that the reward from my training in pursuit of Your Crown fills me to the brim. My steadfast growth and inner beauty is uncontainable. Thank You God for the obstacles that take me from glory to glory. The glory of training for True Royalty lasts forever and I am confident in my invisible crown. I declare that I will lead people to experience the freedom and the joy of the everlasting crown found in You.

Your *Princess*,

Amen.

DAY 42

Status Update: "@SheisMore I am uniquely set apart to carry out an important purpose."
#RiseUpPrincess

I knew you before I formed you in your mother's womb. Before you were born I set you apart...
Jeremiah 1:5

My King,

Before I was conceived in my mother's womb, You knew me. This means that I actually existed before my parents even met. My spiritual self dwelt in heavenly places while You formed every fiber of my being and infused purpose into my heart.

Before I was born, You set me apart from the crowd. I have felt so awkward in groups of people and believed something was wrong with me, but You were actually revealing my uniqueness to me. The qualities that made me feel alienated are actually my greatest gifts. God, thank You for making me a unique princess with a special brand and purpose that no one else can fulfill.

I declare that I will embrace the characteristics that made me feel estranged in the past. When I walk confidently in my uniqueness, I am free to create my best life and I release others to do the same.

Your Princess,

Amen.

DAY 43

Status Update: "@SheisMore I am chosen and called by God to produce good works." #RiseUpPrincess

You did not choose me, but I chose you and appointed you so that you might go and bear fruit—fruit that will last—and so that whatever you ask in my name the Father will give you.
John 15:16

My King and Fruit Bearer,

I am compelled to the core that You not only called me, but You have also appointed me to produce great works. My eyes fill with wonder when I contemplate how important the destiny is You have assigned me. Thank You that I am destined to leave a legacy of love that expands Your Kingdom into unchartered territories and untouched hearts.

Thank You for choosing me and appointing me to transmit beams of hope everywhere I go. My King, I know that all good things flow through centeredness in You. As Your daughter, I will remain humble in order to grow in godly wisdom. Guide me and show me where to sow seeds in nutrient-rich soil.

When I am timid to present my desires and dreams to You, I block Your desire to give me all that I ask. As Your daughter, I have permission to make bold requests in the name of Jesus and to believe whole-heartedly that You will grant them.

I declare that whatever I ask in Your perfect name, you gladly give me! I walk in the purity and love that comes from within and will produce great works where You lead me.

Your *Princess*,

Amen.

DAY 44

Status Update: "@SheisMore I have a destiny mapped out filled with prosperity, hope and goodness." #RiseUpPrincess

For I know the plans I have for you, declares the Lord, plans for welfare and not for evil, to give you a future and a hope.
Jeremiah 29:11

My King and Life Planner,

*S*ometimes I feel like You have forgotten about me. I am overcome by disappointment and discouragement when it feels like I have fallen behind everyone else. Other days, it feels like I am drowning in the hustle of world-changers and I question whether or not I have anything meaningful to contribute.

My King, I declare that those thoughts are from the enemy and I will not let him win by agreeing with his lies. I declare Your promise that says You have plans to prosper me and not to harm me, plans for hope and a future. Thank You for designing me to live a full and prosperous life that I am invited to enjoy in overflowing abundance. Since I trust You, I enjoy my life when things don't seem to be going my way.

I declare that Your amazing plans fall into place in their perfect timing. I live my life in forward motion, but even when life seems to be backwards, I trust You and live expectantly that Your promises will come to pass. You always see me. I am never forgotten.

Your *P*rincess,

Amen.

DAY 45

Status Update: "@SheisMore I have access to the heavenly resources which surround me in the spiritual realm, for I am a citizen of heaven." #RiseUpPrincess

Nor will they say, "Look, here it is!" or "There!" for behold, the kingdom of God is in the midst of you.
Luke 17:21

My King and Confidence,

I am sorry for doubting my divinely-assigned purpose. I get distracted by things like results, numbers, and social media followers, likes and comments. I make the mistake of believing that whoever has the most followers and likes on social media is somehow better than me. I believe that they have more influence and it discourages me because I don't have a platform to gain a large following.

I feel so far behind in catapulting my destiny, but today My King, I take every thought captive. I say no to those lies and realign with the real Truth! Thank You for being so much bigger than social media platforms. Thank You for giving me influence right where I am and I don't need to seek a kingdom anywhere else but within You.

Thank You that I can reach people with my royal influence anywhere I go. When You want to elevate me higher, You will in Your Perfect Timing. Today, I declare that I will live from Your Kingdom in which I live.

Your *Princess*,

Amen.

DAY 46

Status Update: "@SheisMore I have been placed exactly where I am for a specific, royal purpose."
#RiseUpPrincess

For who knows that you have been made queen for such as time as this.
Esther 3:13

My King and Purpose Giver,

*T*hank You that I am right where I am at this very moment for a reason. My life is not a coincidence. The "Godwinks" and "signs" I notice are not by chance. Every piece of my life fits together perfectly, according to Your perfect orchestration. Even when I have de-railed from Your direction, You have still lead me to this very moment. Everything I have gone through has prepared me for *such a time as this.*

My life is heaven-breathed. My life originated as an epic idea in Your Throne Room. Your idea of me is now my royal destiny. I love waking up every day to partner with You in manifesting Your dreams into my reality just like the biblical story Esther. Just as she was entrusted with a royal position so that she might save an entire race, I have also been entrusted with a royal position.

Thank You for strategically placing me right where I am at this very moment for an important time like this. Thank You for being my guide, the Director of my steps. I have been born for a royal purpose beyond my comprehension.

I will act today and be obedient to the royal call on my life. Thank You for the destiny I have been given. As Your princess, I will act every day within my assignment.

Your *P*rincess,

Amen.

DAY 47

Status Update: "@SheisMore I lead with royal integrity so that no one will stumble or find fault with my ministry."
#RiseUpPrincess

We live in such a way that no one will stumble because of us, and no one will find fault with our ministry.
2 Corinthians 6:3

My King and Moral Compass,

*M*any people look up to me and watch my life who I don't even know. Even when I think no one notices, someone is either looking for a reason to follow me or a reason to discredit me. I am grateful for my royal position of leadership because I would rather live in such a way that points others to the True Light than a way that causes them to stumble in the dark.

God, I know that as Your Princess, the stakes are high. My royal destiny isn't worth a night of wild partying or a moment of meaningless pleasure. There are too many lives depending on my leadership and example.

God, I declare that I will royally conduct myself in such a way that inspires others. I am aware that my decisions and actions impact the people around me, not just myself. My life will not cause others to stumble, therefore no one will find fault in my royal ministry, unless it is a lie. Thank You for empowering me to live according to royal standards and to lead a generation by a pure example.

Your *P*rincess,

Amen.

DAY 48

Status Update: "@SheisMore I am prosperous when I refresh others with generosity. #RiseUpPrincess

A generous person will prosper; whoever refreshes others will be refreshed.
Proverbs 11:25

My King and Generous Refresher,

*I*n this society of cut-throat competition, my instinct is to hold my secrets and resources close to me. I am afraid I won't have enough if I share what I have with others. As Your royal daughter, there is no such thing as *not enough*.

You are a God of expansive abundance with a generous spirit. Your Kingdom is like the depth and width of the ocean, always giving and always expanding. There is never a shortage of You. Therefore, when I match up with Your spirit of generosity, I am generating more abundance into the atmosphere.

I declare that I will be the blessing that others pray for. I will be generous with others because I have access to a vault of unlimited riches. I will loosen my grip on control and spread generosity with others. In doing this, I will prosper. You promise that whoever refreshes others will also be refreshed. Thank You that I am refreshed in prosperity when I am generous.

Your *P*rincess,

Amen.

DAY 49

Status Update: "@SheisMore I intend to
speak words that bring life, encouragement
and power." #RiseUpPrincess

The power of life and death is in the tongue.
Proverbs 18:21

My King and Life Speaker,

I devote the words I speak to be encouraging, uplifting and brilliant. You have given me the authority to speak hope and positivity into situations, or the power to speak negativity and fear.

You created the world by speaking. The words you spoke brought life, beauty, creativity and abundance. Since I am made in Your image, the words I speak become my creation as well. God, I declare the words that come out of my mouth will contribute to the royal destiny I intend to live. I will only say things about others that I would want said about me because I am ultimately the only person affected by my private thoughts and words.

As royalty, I will be a leader by inspiring others with my words. I will use my words to *change* a situation rather than to *describe* a situation. I will use my words to *declare Your promises* rather than to *dwell on my problems*. I will speak about things as if they already were and live in such a way that prepares space for blessings and beauty to come into my life.

Your *Princess*,

Amen.

DAY 50

Status Update: "@SheisMore I have
faith in a King that can move
mountains." #RiseUpPrincess

*"You don't have enough faith," Jesus told them. "I
tell you the truth, if you had faith even as small as
a mustard seed, you could say to this mountain,
'Move from here to there,' and it would move.
Nothing would be impossible."*

My King and Master of Faith,

I am so amazed by the power You have given me. I have lived my life by logic and by physical might for so long, but You have made me to be a Princess. I am Your daughter, therefore I get to co-create my dreams with Heaven. We get to work together to leave a legacy on this planet.

I get scared to reach out to people and ask for help. I'd rather do things on my own because I'm afraid no one would believe in me. I am afraid of rejection. I am afraid of letting people down. I question my credibility, my skill and my talent. However, You say when I have faith as small as a mustard seed, I can move mountains. It isn't the most talented woman who gets the job done, it's the one who acts in faith.

God, I trust You. I trust that my dream is not an accident. I trust that You have prepared a path to get there. I trust that when I take action, You will show up in wondrous ways that blow my mind. I declare that when I have faith in You, nothing is impossible. I am born to move mountains and to change the world.

Your *Princess*,

Amen.

DAY 51

Status Update: "I guard my heart with godly wisdom and purify it with forgiveness so that everything that flows from my heart is good."
#RiseUpPrincess

Above all else, guard your heart, for everything you do flows from it.
Proverbs 4:23

My King and Heart Center,

*T*he evidence in my life is a manifestation of the content in my heart. God, I often mistake a lack of self-respect with compassion. I pour out my heart to the people I love only to be met with depreciation and disregard. I allow people to mistreat me over and over again, thinking they will eventually change.

Depression and bitterness each set in my heart when I think about the injustices and hurt I feel. But I do not want toxicity to thrive in my heart because my destiny requires a pure, free and discerning heart. Thank You for showing me that even Jesus set boundaries by only spending time with a solid group of people who believed in him. He gave of Himself and showed compassion, but did not allow ill-intentioned people into His inner circle.

I declare that I will guard my heart against blame and bitterness caused by those who unapologetically take advantage of my kindness. As Your Princess, I will practice Godly wisdom in guarding and protecting my heart so that I will reign with royal purpose in my life.

Your *P*rincess,

Amen.

DAY 52

Status Update: "@SheisMore I let go of relationships that dim my light and surround myself with those who have my best interest at heart." #RiseUpPrincess

So Abram said to Lot, "Please let there be no strife between you and me, nor between my herdsmen and your herdsmen, for we are brothers. "Is not the whole land before you? Please separate from me; if to the left, then I will go to the right; or if to the right, then I will go to the left."
Genesis 3:16-17

My King,

I realize that as Your princess with a royal purpose for my life, my time and well-being is precious. You had a divine calling on Abraham's life and he knew the importance of functioning out of a place of peace. In order for him to be all that You intended him to be, he had to walk away from a toxic relationship. He had to create a healthy space in which to grow.

God, there are some things and even some relationships in my life that are stunting my growth. I don't want to hurt anyone's feelings by cutting them out, but I don't want to compromise my destiny either. My King, I declare that You have amazing plans for the people in my life that I need to let go. I release those people into Your care. God, just as Abraham gave his brother Lot a parting gift, I will also be generous to those I am parting with so they know our time together was valued and appreciated.

I declare that I will let go of the people weighing me down and love them from a distance so that I can weightlessly step into the divine purpose and plans awaiting me.

Your *Princess*,

Amen.

DAY 53

Status Update: "@SheisMore I am blessed when I believe God's promises." #RiseUpPrincess

Blessed is she who has believed that the Lord would fulfill his promises to her!
Luke 1:45

My King and Blesser,

I don't understand why bad things happen to good people. People ask me why I am a Christian when You seemingly don't always protect Your children and it's a hard question to answer. But God, I know that it is in my best interest to never give up on my faith, even when I don't understand the reason unexplainable things happen. It is through the storms that I see Your redeeming rainbow at the end.

Your Word says that I am blessed when I believe You will fulfill your promises to me. Mary, the Mother of Jesus endured ridicule and a tarnished reputation because she believed she would be the Mother of the One True King. It made no logical sense to anyone. She probably felt so alone in her quest, but she didn't give up on her faith and You followed through on Your Promise to her.

I declare that my faith will be as strong as Mary's when I obey Your royal call on my life, even when the road looks dark and lonely. As Your Princess, I know that the rainbow at the end of the storm will be my crowning moment.

Your *Princess*,

Amen.

DAY 54

Status Update: "@SheisMore I am a Daughter of God, therefore I am the head and not the tail, I am at the top and not the bottom." #RiseUpPrincess

The LORD will make you the head, not the tail. If you pay attention to the commands of the LORD your God that I give you this day and carefully follow them, you will always be at the top, never at the bottom.
Deuteronomy 28:13

My King,

Thank You for designing me with the intention to be a woman who blesses others. I'm a woman who leads movements of passion, purity and purpose. Thank You that it is not people who decide who I am or who I am going to be. I am not neglected, I am not overlooked and I am not the root of jokes. Thank You for creating me to be the head and not the tail.

God, I surrender small-thinking and open my mind to divine possibilities. Thank You that when I give my day to You and carefully follow Your footsteps, I will always be at the top and never the bottom.

Today, I declare that I am worthy of being at the top, I am worthy of being followed and I will follow Your instruction even when I am afraid or do not understand. Thank You for guiding me with Your voice and Your commands that serve to protect me. Through my obedience and faith, the divine destiny on my life will be fulfilled.

Your Princess,

Amen.

DAY 55

Status Update: "@SheisMore I am provided for by the glorious riches I have inherited as His Daughter." #RiseUpPrincess

And my God will supply every need of yours according to his riches in glory in Christ Jesus.
Philippians 4:19

My King and Glorious Supplier,

*T*oday, I cast every worry and anxious thought upon Your Throne. I know my thoughts impact my feelings, which ultimately lead to my actions. Your Word says that You will supply every one of my needs according to *Your* glorious riches. I am not inhibited by logic or financial constraints.

Thank You I never have to worry about having enough. Thank You when I believe Your promise for abundance, I feel empowered and free to take action on my purpose. Thank You God for seeing all of my needs, even the ones I haven't noticed yet. Thank You for knowing my needs in advance and always having a path prepared for me. You give me the means to get there and an open door. Your resources are exceeding, immeasurable and infinite. I receive all that You have for me with gratitude. Thank You for always giving me more than enough.

Right now, I relinquish the burdens I am not meant to carry and I receive Your promise of overflowing provision with open hands and a thankful heart. Today, I expect to see divine surprises that will cover my needs, because You love me that much.

Your *P*rincess,

Amen.

DAY 56

Status Update: "@SheisMore I am a co-heir to the Son of God and I share in His glory." #RiseUpPrincess

Now if we are children, then we are heirs-heirs of God and co-heirs with Christ. If indeed we share in His sufferings in order that we may also share with His glory.
Romans 8:17

My King,

The gravity of the inheritance I have in You is stunning. It's wondrous to wrap my mind around the fact that I get all of the same powers, promises and glory as Jesus did. He suffered in death so I could be Your royal daughter, so I could have the chance to know You intimately like He did. Since I am a co-heir with Christ, that means I can operate in all of the same spiritual gifts, peace, joy and confidence, as when He walked the earth.

Jesus was persecuted, accused and ridiculed for years, yet he was a constant pillar of strength. His enemies did not stop him from carrying out His mission to bring justice to the world. Persecution didn't stop Him from healing people and restoring hearts. Since I am His co-heir, I have that same ability to be resilient to my enemies and to take risks in manifesting Your beautiful call on my life. I know that when I live in alignment with You, I will share in similar sufferings.

I declare that even when I'm afraid, staying true to my royal identity and purpose is worth the pain inflicted by people who still live in darkness. Thank You God that when I share in the sufferings of Christ, I also get to share in the greater reward of Your glory.

Your Princess,

Amen.

DAY 57

Status Update: "@SheisMore I am a victor. Through Him, the battle has already been won." #RiseUpPrincess

No, in all these things we are more than conquerors through him who loved us.
Romans 8:37

My King and Conqueror,

J am so grateful that You have predestined me to be an overcomer. You chose my family, my birth order, my genetics and my generational blessings. Some parts of my life are fabulous, but other parts have inflicted scars on my heart. Thank You that every puzzle piece from my parents, my siblings, my body type, my talents, my setbacks and even my geographical location has been interwoven magnificently for Your royal intention.

Your plans are more powerful than anything that has ever served as a setback. Since I am Your chosen daughter, Your kingdom lives within me and I have already won any battle before it has even begun. Thank You God that through You, I am more than a conqueror.

I declare I am a warrior princess that puts on my spiritual armor every morning so that no weapon formed against me will ever prosper. I can be peaceful through the storm because I know that victory already has my name on it. Thank You God that I am more than a conqueror in life because of Your Love.

Your *P*rincess,

Amen.

DAY 58

Status Update: "@SheisMore I will accomplish my dreams with a spirit of power, love and self-discipline."
#RiseUpPrincess

For God has not given us a spirit of fear and timidity, but of power, love, and self-discipline.
Timothy 1:7

My King,

I have ideas that could change the world around me. I have natural gifts and talents to bring them to life. The only thing stopping me from manifesting my ideas into an inspiring reality is myself.

God as Your princess, You have equipped me with every spiritual ability to fulfill my dream. A spirit of fear and laziness is for those who partner with the enemy. I am partnered with the God of the Universe. I am commissioned to co-create with my God who gives me a spirit of power, love and self-discipline.

My King, I am Your warrior princess. Nothing can stop me on the path to reign with divine purpose and dreams. When I am tempted to quit, I will remember that I am not a quitter. When I want to pull back in fear, I will remember that I have a spirit of power. When I want to fall back on hateful self-talk, I will remember that I have a spirit of love that covers all wrongs.

I declare that I will be bold in asking for help, powerful in my intentions and disciplined in the commitment it takes to be excellent. I am born to win, so I will prepare to win and expect to win.

Your *Princess*,

Amen.

DAY 59

Status Update: "@SheisMore I am clothed in the full armor of God, the enemy doesn't stand a chance against me." #RiseUpPrincess

Therefore put on the full armor of God, so that when the day of evil comes, you may be able to stand your ground, and after you have done everything, to stand. Stand firm then, with the belt of truth buckled around your waist, with the breastplate of righteousness in place, and with your feet fitted with the readiness that comes from the gospel of peace. In addition to all this, take up the shield of faith, with which you can extinguish all the flaming arrows of the evil one. Take the helmet of salvation and the sword of the Spirit, which is the word of God.
Ephesians 6:13-17

My King,

I am a target to the enemy because I am infused with purpose for Your Kingdom. My dreams are precious and I will not attain them without experiencing resistance. Setbacks do not mean that I am supposed to quit, they mean I am supposed to keep pressing in with recharged faith and royal ferocity.

I can't fight the devil's strategies and schemes on my own. He will use people, finances, and my own ego to taunt me and tear me down. I will not go out into the world until I have fully coated myself in the armor of God.

I know that the struggle isn't between people, but against the spiritual rulers and forces of wickedness. I will not empower their tactics with timidity or be pierced by their spiritual weaponry. I will turn away from the cloud of evil and become immune when I put on the whole armor of Light.

I declare I wear the belt of truth that rebukes the father of lies. My breastplate of righteousness is in place and my feet bring peace to moments of confusion. I carry the shield of faith that deflects all doubt and I hold up the sword of the Spirit. I declare I am coated in Your royal armor and the enemy has no chance against me.

Your *Princess*,

Amen.

DAY 60

Status Update: "@SheisMore I focus on what God can do, not on what I can not do. When I step out in faith, the impossible happens." #RiseUpPrincess

The Lord will grant that the enemies who rise up against you will be defeated before you. They will come at you from one direction but flee from you in seven.
Deuteronomy 28:7

My King and Warrior,

I declare that no threat, setback or attack will cause me to quit. As a daughter after Your own heart, my enemies are caused to flee from me in seven directions. God, I will focus on Your supernatural strength and power rather than my limitations and problems. I will focus on what You can do instead of what I can not do.

In the natural, I may not have the most talent, the most money or the most influence. But in the supernatural, I have the God of the Universe crushing obstacles and preparing a way with smooth transitions and divine acceleration. My King, when I live my life according to Your perfect commands, there will be no space for the enemy to thrive in my life.

I live above the entrapment of self-hate, self-doubt, eating and drinking, low energy, substances and toxic relationships. As Your princess, I walk in Your Light and Your face shines upon me. Today, I will purposefully set my hands on creating my dreams and I will set my mind on Your ability to take them places beyond my imagination.

Your *Princess,*

Amen.

Congratulations Princess! Your 20 Day *She Reigns* journey is complete! Seal your destiny in the contract below:

I, _____, am committed to reigning in life as His Princess. I know that I am destined to live a royal purpose in order to leave a royal legacy for the world. I am fully equipped to do every good work He has called me to do because I live in His Kingdom. God's Kingdom is abundant, limitless and exceeds my imagination.

I am committed to take action every day within my royal assignment even when I am afraid. I intend to stay focused, disciplined and steadfast in my race to carry out my destiny. I will seek wisdom so I will know when to serve and when to lead. I will surround myself with others who uplift me and believe in my mission.

I will lead with kingdom integrity. I was born to win, so I will prepare to win and plan to win.

My royal identity *Reigns* with purpose.

For more resources to
deepen and enrich your
royal journey, you are
invited to
SheisMore.com.

Kristen Dalton Wolfe

Kristen Dalton Wolfe is Miss USA 2009 and the Founder of SheisMore.com, a faith-based online women's magazine that reaches thousands of women worldwide. With a big sister's heart as the oldest of 4 children, she has dedicated her life to "raising up princesses" by revealing our royal identity in Christ. The mission of She is More is to Reveal True Identity, Radiate Inner Beauty & Confidence, and Reign with Purpose.

Kristen leads a women's bible study in Los Angeles and shares a motivational speaking company with her husband Kris, Founder of GoodGuySwag.com. They also host a podcast show on iTunes called, *Relationships Radio*.

Kristen majored in Psychology and Spanish at East Carolina University. As a renaissance woman with a love for the performing arts, Kristen also models & acts in Hollywood and is the National Spokesmodel for LA Fitness & appears in multiple national commercials. She and her husband Kris have a vision for revolutionizing a generation of men and women to rise up to their true identities and ultimately cultivating healthy & loving relationships.

To Book Kristen for Your Event, visit: www.SheisMore.com/BookKristen

Made in the USA
Middletown, DE
29 November 2016